On Long Mountain

for Anne Hobson Freeman
and in memory of Mina

Contents

On Long Mountain

PERSEID NIGHT

The storm of stars predicted
can't break this clouded sky, so in my
pulled-up chair on Long Mountain
I give up the sight—and begin to hear
the storm of sounds that pelt the air:
chirp and drill and drum and vibrato,
rhythmic rasp and blue-note howl.
Meteors of messages
trace quick arcs across me.
Now and then a barking dog
from down at Bluford's. And I understand
the crickets, a cow's low call, mosquito whine.
But it's so dark to a city girl
sitting out here to see stars—
What makes a shriek? a chuff? a tinny cry?
Who is signaling, what is signed?
Are any getting answers beneath this no-show heaven?

UNARMED

Get a gun was what was offered
as advice
by all but the closest friend
who said
You'd shoot yourself. Out of stupidity.
Or sadness.

In the Blue Ridge Mountain cabin loft
lying awake alone
I stare at the timbered ceiling
—and because I believed her—
fight fear unarmed.

For a long time the bear
scratched her nails on the windowpane,
muffled her thumps at the door,
shifted her shape under barnlight.

So too the hiker crazed for the food
of my flesh, swings my rust-hinged gate,
scrapes his knife against the tin roof,
strangles soft things into tiny shrieks.

While the snake, the copperhead,
slides along the rafter,
dangles over my head in my fitful sleep,
eases back into shadow when I jerk awake and reach

for the gun
that I never got, so much more afraid
of stupidity, of sadness.

Calligraphy of a
Virginia Night

8:50, June, from across the road
> *as soon as I hang them clothes up*
> *y'all goin to bed!*
door slam, hog grunts,
mockingbird, rooster,
child squeal
> *git outta there Poke-chop!*
door slam

9:00, silence at Bluford's

9:05, from a long way off,
from across black-on-black hills,
way beyond Bluford's
> *Mommie! Mommie! Mommie!*
> *WHAT!*

9:10, sudden quiet—
just like that, just like light going,
noise goes

9:25, traces across silence—
the distant trucks on sixty
one dog barking near
one dog barking far—
oh, now a screen door bangs
sharp but normal

someone's in or out at Bluford's,
maybe a last load of clothes to hang
now that things have quieted down.

Down in the Shenandoah Valley
Cy Twombly's come home,
he says, "like an old dog."

This graffiti's expensive too:
there are times of night I'd give my life
to hear it pricking out the dark.

HOLE IN THE GROUND

Under the raspberry bush, under the dogwood,
here and there in the grassy lawn,
up by the house, down by the stream
are the holes.

The last redoubts of my fears are so simple.
Holes. Holes in the ground.

Understand, grandchildren (when you can you
can), old friends, family, any man who
thinks of me from time to time—
I'm doing fine up here on Long Mountain,
up here in the Blue Ridge.

I've pushed my mushy fears
down into holes of my own digging,
planted my racing heart with the bleeding heart—
that hardy fort to rabbits and drought.
I've planted fear's little ache with the brave
hollyhock, the wary eye with the wide-eyed
Susan, the wild thoughts deep
with the tubers of wild blue iris.
Hole after hole.

I got cats for the mice
D-Con for the rats
A strong barn light that comes on
by itself when it senses the night.
A big clunky lock for the gate.

But out here this hot, clear morning—
unhazed for a change in July—I
step free of the unexpected,

plunge into underbrush, pick
the thick raspberries just to eat.
Then I see the hole at my feet.

There is no doubt what its circumference is like.

OVER AFTON

The driving lesson calls for us to drive
across the Blue Ridge: from Richmond west
to Charlottesville, then over Afton Mountain,
and down into the Shenandoah Valley.

The will-be driver is asleep, his hair
against the window turning gold, his smooth
cheek gleamed by summer sun. "Wake up," I say,
"You've got to be alert." I touch his wrist
that's never moved from birth; he has to learn
to drive a custom car without his hands.
He stirs and grumbles with closed eyes, "Ah, Mom,
just let me sleep until we're there, okay?"

BE ALERT WHEN FOG IS ON THE MOUNTAIN
the yellow signs proclaim on this blue day.
When I was twenty no sign said a word.
I drove the two-lane blacktop over Afton
in midnight dark, a dozen fogs, to see
the father of this sleeping boy. And on
those times he drove me home to Roanoke,
I hoped for Afton's tricks to slow us down.

One winter's trick was played on me alone:
a sudden cap of storm and thick fast snow.
The air was white, the highway white, the edge
of Afton disappeared. The wipers froze.
Afraid to stop, I reached around and jerked
the wiper from the ice with my bare hand,
but then it wouldn't move without its mate.

I rubbed a hole, another, then another,
a hole on white, soon closed with darker white.

I knew I'd started going down—the slant
inside my car the only clue—and that
the cliff was near, the precipice of Afton
on my right. I geared to first and tried
to breathe, believing this white field I plowed
could now be even with the railing.
A foot ahead was all that I could see:
faint tracks of tires that kept on being there.
What made them I would come to at the bottom—
the jackknifed truck that led me over Afton.

This morning patchwork fields light up below us.
A sign says tourists may pull off and park
to walk up to the guardrail and look down.
If I had slid off Afton in that whiteout,
I would have hit this morning's SCENIC VIEW,
dropped on Nelson County like a boulder,
a mound of metal on the country road
where signs insist WATCH OUT FOR FALLEN ROCKS.

I turn a dial and blast the air with rock
to wake him up as we speed down and pass
the backs of signs that warn the Eastbound lane.
Madonna urges all the world's new drivers:
GO FAST, MAKE LOVE, HAVE FUN, BE FREE. "Okay!"
I shout, "we're almost over Afton, almost there."
And he sits up and grins because we are.

Two cool days turn a few leaves red on one dogwood
and even though every leaf in my yard is green—
maple, azalea, maidenhair fern, ginkgo,
gardenia, pin oak, willow—
these scarlet few are a fingernail
on my shoulderblade.
I turn
to push the duffle into his trunk,
help to hoist the mystery box,
leave all the dollars in my wallet
on the dashboard,
smile red goodbyes
to the packed back, the convivial stickers.
The dust in the driveway drifts toward the trees,
yards full, woods full, all dull green
except that tip of dogwood waving too.

LETTER TO CONRAD

Thanks for the poem
called *Fork*. Your words wind
through the tines
of that most familiar ware
like notes on a staff making music.

They remind me
of the time we strolled by a fork—
a *prong* of the river it used to be called—
listened as it tuned, sat for
our picture on a wooden footbridge.
Mary Page clicked us smiling
in March sun with daffodils
by this fork that begins in a spring
on Long Mountain
and promised us Spring
as it played on its way to the James.

But didn't you leave out
the fork we forgot to beware?
You know the one, that tongue
that flicks in our ear—
whispering over and over
how easy it is to be happy?

GNAT FACTS ON NPR

Now I know for sure
every living thing springs
for sex. Gnats
swarming in your face
snuffing up your nose
guttering in the liquid of your eye—
they're doing a fucking *dance*!
Their aerial male fandango's as hot
as Watusi writhing in fireheat,
as white boys oiling their torsos
to volley a ball at Fort Lauderdale.
"They orient themselves to a tall pole"
says here—which is you, in June,
gnat-exasperated, batting hot air—
"and if that pole moves—they go with it."
Down the graveled walk by the black walnut
where you wanted to talk, to maybe touch,
but you're fanning your sweaty face,
your lips are sealed.
It's all for the females,
says the expert, who "hang back on the sidelines
until the frenetic cloud of their kind
is too much to resist." Then they jump in—
mate right there in your shut-down face.

It's the radio's word *sidelines*
switches the picture to cold Friday nights,
the sidelines swaying to rhythmic cheers,
the scrimmagers wild in a flurry of motion's
sounds: tackle and crack and knocked-out wind.
Then something signals us girls. A buzzer, a gun,

and it's time to run
onto the field, into the thick, grab the boys tight
around stiff plastic pads, thin padded hips,
knowing their swarming is all about *us,*
loving the sweat they drip.

WAYS TO GO

Let us go then you and I . . .
　　—T. S. Eliot

There's a hell of a good universe next door;
　　Let's go!
　　　—e.e. cummings

Let's go to Gubbio tonight.
　　—William Matthews

How casually poets and people use
"Let's go"—as if it were a given
that someone else will want to.

On the drive to Gubbio, she'll sigh
at that sunset behind the ancient towers
and hills of Tuscany. He'll feel, with her hand on
his thigh, it's okay to think about religion
and her breasts rounded above the peasant blouse.

Not that "Let's go" is always a poet's dream.
The pasta could be at Joe's on Route 1,
or the words sighed by two
who're bored with Chesterfield County.
They may even be bored with each other
as they open the doors to their car.

But the singular construction cannot invite
a soul to come along.
Its whole tone is joyless,
breaking someone's hold, insisting
on leaving for Italy alone.

Her words still ring in the roadway:
"Let me go, let me go."

SENSING WINTER

Four narcissus blooms, browning
paper-whites forced for Christmas,
assert their scents like skunks
on the cold night parkway.
In a small apartment there's no doubt
what wins among the senses.
The silent telephone smells
like plastic when the handle of a pan
melts over the burner turned to high.
The woman stretches out of her sweater,
unbuttons her wool skirt that falls
around her feet. She hooks her thumbs
into her pantyhose, watches her body
becoming naked in the mirror
propped against a wall. She shivers in
the forced-air heat and for a second
she can smell her skin, its sweetness.
But her own odor won't linger here,
faint as the tentative fingertip
she touches to her self.

LIKE YOUNG MEN

It's hard not to love
the way they stand, easy and affirmed
like young men alone together
not knowing they're watched.

A sweetness in their power, a hesitancy.
One stag lowers his head to my garden.
The other, calmly alert, looks to this cabin.

They take turns protecting each other
in a beautiful simplicity of eating and guarding.
Their clay-colored bodies are a massive surprise
after the delicate doe I've chased from here.

Their racks are young, but sharpening. It's hard
not to stare, not to freeze. The guardian
arouses the other to a scent of harm
that could be me—

his antlers toss and almost instantly
both deer bound up the hill,
take my fence with ease,
lithe and cocky as teenagers, armed.

EVEN IN FOXES

Even in foxes
cunning and quickness
curl in on themselves
in the den of that thief, time.

Brain and bones click into pain
in the loose bag dimmed to dun.
Each bristle wilts,
limp as an eyelash.

At the henhouse stupidity clucks
among the young
who misunderstand
the hand that feeds them,

while on the hill the jangling hounds
call out their longing,
sniffing the air, the ground,
confused by the musk of memory.

VALDOSTA

How do I like it here?
I've been young so long, being here
is taking some adjustment. At first
the squared-off lowrise blocks, expected stop-
lights regulating traffic,
the sunlight on brick buildings
looked familiar.
A Hopper afternoon, I thought, or downtown
Valdosta in the fifties.

After a while you get tired of adjusting,
weary so soon on the afternoon errand,
moving with care like one under water, though air
dries your eyes beyond blinking
and the sunlight glares glass into mirrors.

So it's a mystery who's inside cars,
and what's behind storefront windows.
Who is that girl in the tight black shorts
cross-cutting traffic like a lawless god?
The grace of her bare long legs, the freedom
of her unbound breasts, is she running to that shadow
in the alley? She flings open her arms to something
or somebody there, her reckless hair
glints sun like chrome.

Stopped like everyone else on this street,
I see her quick motion reflect in the glass,
then disappear, and I hate it here, I hate it.

CAUGHT AGAIN

Not red-handed but red-wined
leaving the place with no lights
caught to walk
the unsteady line.

No lights here now
either. Except the blueblinks
and flash beam
in my face.

I have been very bad
says the dream replayed.

Take this, says the cop
offering his hand
to hit me.

His partner turns on
his car's interior light,
to write.

My life blinks out in blue
off-on, off-on.
In this cold car I picture
the warmest I've ever been.
Alone at the wheel. One man
at the window, offering his hand.
Nearby, a man writing
under a small steady light.

MOON ARRANGEMENT

Moisture goes—
across the arc of the eye,
the valley of the thighs;
elbow and eyelid, lips and cheeks
parch into drought lines
designing the skin into reminders
of the end of plums, of Auden, of roses
in a dried arrangement.

The mouths of the body remember rivers
but do not weep into seas, or suck, or slide
the long boats into the harbors.
While under this surface we're wetlands—
marsh dark beneath the winter reeds
that click and rattle at the moon.

And month after month that moon's surface
lights the wind-bent sedge,
the hollow pods, the flakes of seed.
And month after month that magnet moon
powers our dark waters
as if we were still an ocean.

NAMELESS

The vagina did not have a name at all
before 1700.
   —Stephen Jay Gould

vagina—from the Latin: sheath, scabbard.
   —*Oxford English Dictionary*

Most all of us came this way.
Muscled through the no-name,
our big heads stretched the holding tight
that still presses our bodies in dreams.

Even the gentle lover finds no object
for his verb to whisper as he enters
the holding tight that presses like his dreams.
The route of his birth and his fathering
is not sealed at the end of his penis,
is neither sheath nor scabbard.

And some who died to tell about it speak
in similes: of darkness like a corridor,
like a tunnel, like a narrow passageway
to brilliance.

They can't compare their going out
with the birth they don't remember,
and even if near death they could,
the route has no true name.

Momentary Travels

I had thought these moments were yours,
these moments when I've left this life
for that other one, I thought you were there too.

That everybody was there. That this
was where you all went
when I couldn't find you.

But I just now suspected you might be
at your own places—not this one
Thelonious Monk drifted me into

before sleep where I'm around midnight,
young and sultry at a corner table
in a dark and smoky jazz club.

In of course New York.
But were you in the Shenandoah Valley
that redbud April afternoon?

There was a trout stream there,
a little stream, but noisy as jazz
in the smoky air of the Blue Ridge.

I've begun to think the sadness
that wells up in me when I return
is that I was never there, myself.

A Walk Back to Hollins

for Wyndham

It's growing dark as two young women
look up to the mountains,
familiar Tinker Mountain, a charcoal ark
against the violet sky.
The path is darkening too through leafless trees
where the friends walk close in bulky coats.
They can see the breath their rapid words
are forming in cold air,
but not what else that I see there,
the pathways branching fast in their young minds.
They'd laugh to call their conversation learning—
the way they laugh at something one just said.
I hear that lilting sound become an echo
as one reaches for the other's arm,
though neither is afraid—I know this now—
that she will lose her way.
Across the dark they see their destination,
and I wish with all my heart to go there with them:
all the library's lights are coming on,
silhouetting ancient oak trees,
shining through the maze of lifting branches.

LONG MOUNTAIN OTTER

for Temple Martin

He is not really local, not
a Long Mountain otter—
or for that matter,
though he seems to be
smoothly furred in the curved stone,
he's neither sleek nor wet.

But he looks wet.
As if he'd slipped out of water, not
been chiseled from dry stone.
Maybe he's not a Long Mountain otter,
but an animal yet to be
named, a whole new matter.

The *heart* of the matter,
really. In a dust-filled barn, wet
life emerges, begins to be
what can breathe, not
only in water and in air, but an otter
that takes breath in stone.

It could be a stone
from Long Mountain, as a matter
of fact, rolled to where the slick otter
slides his trout along the wet
rocks to live in the air as we do, not
underwater where he could choose to be.

It even could be
that once an otter clambered up this very stone,
forsaking the grace of water to take in the air. Not

that it matters.
It is only this stone that makes him wet.
Only Temple makes him this otter.

Temple is the sculptor of the otter,
she's the one who made him be
quick and sleekly furred and wet.
In the waters of my mind the heaviest stone
swims lithely and everything that matters
moves, alive or not.

Born wet out of stone,
it doesn't matter what he's not.
The Long Mountain Otter is freed to be.

Painting the Blue Ridge Red

Art class assignment: use opposite hues.
So undulant mountains
blued by the haze their humid greens give off
are red as ocean rollers in a sunrise.
Look at my bluebird almost orange
and that ripening corn—a mustard field.
I'll make the lilac brown and tinge
the cows with pink. The chinking
of the cabin I'll turn purple.
But wait awhile, Long Mountain paints
this exercise itself: cadmium trees,
alizarin ridges. Lilac dries to burnt sienna,
the greens of summer go to ochre.
The goldfinch molts to gray.
In winter light, the cabin
casts its violet shadow. Here
no color can surprise a canvas
except crow's constancy.

SWING, BOAT, TABLE

What Hanno has made of wood this year:
a swing, a boat, a table.

He doesn't believe he's made art this year;
the swing, the boat, the table

are objects he made to invite those he loves
to sit down.

Not objects people in rooms walk around,
regard in boredom or awe while locked at the knee—

a few vaguely yearning to float to the sea,
break bread with friends, rise through the air—

a few vaguely yearning—and not knowing why—
to sit in a tree.

POETRY READING

This is my last poem:
pay attention.
I know there were minutes—
whole poems back there—
when I lost you.
I know your mind tried, for a while,
to stay behind your eyes
but at times, it just had to be excused
as I used to raise my hand and
ask Miss Sanders, *May I?*
And out I'd go, excused
from the overheated room,
the drone of geography, the smell
of bananas in brown paper bags,
and though Tammy tried to come with me
it was always one-at-a-time
just as *your* mind couldn't leave this room
with the mind of that person sitting beside you
(try as you might to invite it along)
but walked down the hall by itself
into that small hotel
where some word I'd spoken
—hibiscus, vanilla, mahogany, snow—
reminded you
someone you've missed for a very long time
stands at a window brushing her hair
and hearing you speak her name she turns
her face that has not changed at all
to yours and holds out her arms to encircle your body
which is not there, but here in this room
where you've sat very still and listened
to some if not all of my words
and may or may not have heard
that this is my last poem.

"Willem de Kooning
Declared Incompetent"

—news item, August, 1989

Experts sent to inspect him assert
he can't tell the difference between one and a million.
But "de Kooning continues to paint every day."

In conversation he roamed from the subject
of money. It's all potatoes
Willem de Kooning declared, incompetent.

He looks out at the level potato field,
at the straight line it makes with the Long Island sky
and the line that it doesn't make with the sky—
the line of his mind that he makes as de Kooning
continues to paint
every day.

THE LININGS OF TUNNELS,
THE UNDERSIDES OF ROOFS

Since the mid-19th century the people of Sunset Park have earned
their livings making the linings of tunnels, the undersides of
roofs, ships' propellers, insulation materials, wiring, everything
unseen.
   —Roger Rosenblatt

Who'd stop traffic in the Hampton Roads Tunnel—
the kids hot and cranky in back—to inspect the lining
that holds our breath under water?

Or would you be willing to climb up and check
beneath shingles, the slate, the fake cedar shakes,
what undersides keep out the storm? You knew
your roof was nailed to something.

I saw a ship's propeller high in the air,
drying out in the sun at the shipyard.
So still, a bird
balanced on one of its blades.
But to see one churn, working well, is a peril.
We stand above it, going somewhere.

Our insulation from freezing is famous,
foamed batting snugged
between our walls,
our ceilings and floors, where
the wiring is hidden as well,
branching around us in secret.

Though wiring eventually
comes into view, threads our houses
and poles in plain air, straight

down narrowing streets of perspective
to connect us to power and words.

But it's clear now that wire will disappear too.
Circuitous filaments so fine, so tiny, wire's work
will be done invisibly—
like fingertips turning a lining
that no one will ever see
in someplace up north called Sunset Park.

UFFIZI EXPLOSION

May 27, 1993

Looking down on Florence
Savaronala saw it
as a finale.

Fragments flew skyward
heavier than air,
heavier than smoke, than ashes.

Shreds of iron, leaded glass,
canvas and marble
ascended a second then crashed.

Thick shards of mortar
flung and sunk,
stone on stone.

I lost, he thought.
*Fire is too beautiful
to consume art.*

*It takes boom and weight
the ugly trashing
no bonfire can make—*

*man's vanity
in pieces at last
in my piazza.*

Morning of Words

It's not the crack of dawn
                    but crows
that crack open black beaks
                       to hawk
raw calls to first light.

If day breaks
                the cock's broken crowing
mixes the message.

Dawn itself has risen
              up through the soup of words
to mean perception—

Look it's the sun! Come round hallelujah
again!—
                and it's dawned
on us that day doesn't break,
                    or crack,
that words bear the history of ignorance.

                    But even enlightened,
believing Galileo,
                we've locked him away
from our language,

and alone in the dark
                I can't say out loud

              the sun never rises.

STAYED

So you have stayed, all these years
with the one who grew large, whose shape
in the space beside you made you shrink,
whose body filled your house like a balloon
pressing softly against your face, your mouth,
your hands, your back—those days you turned to me
who was slim and lithe as an aspen, then.

So too I have stayed, all these years
with the shape beside me fattening and plush,
swelling over most of the mattress, crowding
my kitchen so I can hardly open the oven door.
When I try to turn around, I'm enveloped
in stuff soft as dough. I know
how you felt, then, though I live alone.

Can't You Hear Me
Singing, Alfred Prufrock?

I watched you today in my mind's eye—
walk down the stairs,
your rumpled pants rolled at the ankle
your bald spot round as a target.
You were going. And what's more,
dying. Or going
to die. *Wait!* I yelled,
I'm going too!
You stopped, popeyed as a lobster:
Do I understand just what you mean?
Of course, I said, and in an instant
we were sitting
in an orchard on Long Mountain
laughing, dying
laughing and eating
peaches, touching each
other with warm sticky fingers.

BLUES IN THE BLUE RIDGE

On the year's hottest day
Wynton Marsalis trumpets a dirge
over the burial beat
of a New Orleans drum.

Under the clicking ceiling fan
I'm reading Euripides,
sweating in my white nightgown,
the thinnest cotton I brought up here
to pass this time alone.
The fan sends its heated breeze
to my wicker chair.

It's afternoon in August; in Argos
Electra is mourning her father,
keening her dark lamentation,
her rhythmical, murderous song.

This bleaching sun in Virginia
bears down on the mountainside,
the grass is as dry and as dun as Mycenae's.
Goldfinches fight over thistle. Sunflowers glare.
In this thick air my thin batiste gown
sticks to the sides of my breasts.
I can barely move
in the heat and light of grief
as mourners in New Orleans wail
in hot black suits and blues.

At Epidaurus

Our little tribe
twenty or so
from the old New World
sat in a segment of curve
on the first two rows
of stone.

September had emptied
the ancient theater
cut into the pine groves
on Mount Kynortion,
though a summer sun
still burned down
from cloudless blue
over Mycenae and Argos,
over us.

We leaned into each other
for shade and to listen
to the one man among us
who knew the old words.

Alone in the center
of the packed-earth round,
he recited the poetry
of Euripides:
the longing of Phaedra
to be right and do wrong—
though nobody, not
even the guides from Nauplia,
knew that Greek
that struck passion
on reason like match
on stone.

Still,
unruly children
got quiet.
A few tourists testing
the famous acoustics,
even two stonecutters
at work by the exit
(listening to rock
on a yellow radio)
grew quiet

as his unintelligible words
flickered into rhythm
then rose like the flame
from Olympus
one runner keeps lit.

While around us,
behind us
across the sun-struck stage
the empty stone rows
ranged up to the sky like years

strictly attending to what
they've come down to.

Swimming in the Aegean

If you do the dead man's float
and open your eyes
you will be blinded by a blueness
full of light.

Sometimes we're not meant to see.
When everywhere you look
mythic murder is visual news:
a woman axes her husband
three thousand years ago,
a man slaughters his wife,
pulling her head back by the hair
to expose her throat
like a sacrifice.

On television, on pediments,
hatred with its different handsome faces
claims the same scrubby land.

Or I see a woman like me,
shopping for a particular fish,
extinguished in a firestorm
in Pompeii, in Sarajevo.

After the delicate richness of frescoes,
the rawness of flesh, fat packed
in garish shirts, after
gold and lapis bracelets
smooth as the slippery limestone
gleamed by a million feet into marble,
after the crowded climb to the empty temple—
back at the sheet-white houses on Idra, even,
in the lattice-dappled restaurant, too

many thin cats, too
many thin dogs stalk our scraps.

Then perhaps it's a blessing
to float face down—
your eyes stung by nothing but salt—
looking as long as one held breath
at nothing but blue.

ORACLE

Wonder is what Delphi's all about:
I wonder, you wonder
he, she, it wonders
and we all would climb a mountain
to find out—
all of you, and they, would pack a bus
a donkey, a chariot for one and retinue,
to wind up that steep and dangerous road
(where, if you wreck, you get a small shrine
as this century leaps to conclusion)
to arrive at wonder—
to come to your senses and know
the sacred in a sky that beams
its white heat or hides,
to gaze down the wide sweep
of water or trees to a sea
that is either the color called "winedark"
or blue
when what I want and you do is *yes*.
Or *no. Stop.* Or *Go.*
Is a god there?
Is *there?*
What is coming.
We climb up to Delphi over and over,
answering our hearts with olive leaves dancing
now silver, now gray, now sunstruck green—
old motionless mountainflow
down to what seems like the sea.

"Now Words Are
Surrounded by Spaces"

—elementary Classical Greek textbook

To me it hadn't occurred
that words were
surrounded by spaces

that once
ancient Greek ran words like pearls
able to touch each other's curves
across the knotted string
each one gleaming
like strung round worlds
by Vermeer

that somewhere
along the line
someone
split words in two like the axed dash
of Emily Dickinson

and now the space that surrounds
a word
can hold it like a star
in darkness
the space between words
can gape and take
my stepping foot to a place
I hadn't planned.

Was it safer when nouns
held on tight
to what moved them through space:

backward or forth
to what lands or latches or catches
or is
an object?

Oh words how unhooked you've become after Greek!
Look at you standing there
side by side
straining so hard to make meaning,
pretending you've never touched.

Who Plays Your Piano?

You say when it was new
the keys broke cleanly.
Now the ivories fuse
like mending bone.

Thick ink of Chopin
clouds on the rack,
sonatas balked by
soldered intervals.

The alphabet is all you'll learn
from shelved encyclopedias—
behind each spine compacted worlds
are losing definition.
Atoms of Aristotle swirl into Arcturus,
Audubon's welded to automobile.
Something you meant to know has changed.

Or consider the Concorde:
for the price of a piano
three extra hours in Paris ticked
in francs like a taxi
while you slept in the Hilton, alone.

Once a man old enough to be your father
loved you. Once a boy young as a son.
They looked into your opaque eyes
as I do now.

But it's impossible, you say,
turning away, paying again
for this expensive air.

FAMILY LIFE

$500 for a single poem with the theme of "family
bliss and failure"
—contest announced in
Poets & Writers Magazine, June, 1996

This—
brown-haired boy, ambling up a mountainside,
picking a tune on his banjo, his little daughter
making her own way on lamb's legs
through the thick April grass.
And they're mine: boy, baby, I
can even claim the framing:
air, sun, bluegrass tune, scent of pear tree
barely blooming, those pale green poplars
mending winter ridges.
This railing I am leaning on.
This woven moment
holding time
around me like a nest.
Bliss—
five hundred dollars is not enough
for me to tell the rest.

ATLANTA

Atlanta lies hot and almost tropical
after summer rains.
Inside the tall cold slabs of buildings
air-conditioned glaze paints out
the ghosts on the asphalt, rising
up each afternoon from the steaming puddles.

In our lingerings
between the air-cooled cars and the crisp interiors—
the damp-backed good-byes on our parents' driveway—
heat haze rises around our ankles,
assuming shapes that make us sweat.

It is usually Mother, hot and amorphous as ever,
embarrassing our bare legs.
She presses to tell us she was steamed to death
by Atlanta, not by the doctors' cold conclusion
in the steely room.

At one time or another our other parents,
great or grand, visit the only hot places
left in Atlanta, wilting our Buckhead
haircuts, our Sea Island cottons, whispering
stay out, stay out here . . .
we will tell you a story . . .

Some afternoons we do. Lost
in listening, we lean on the cars, slap at our ankles.
then talk about growing up in Atlanta, how we kept cool:
the ratcheting attic fan, the shuttered rooms, mint
iced tea, cold chicken, cold tomato aspic—

The menu summons those old ghosts who served it,
black as the charred earth we were born on.

We make lame jokes; they bite—
sting our skin like sweat bees
then rise above the ground and us like smoke.

That's when we flee inside—not unlike Yankees
closing windows and doors to their chill
Maine fogs, their Boston blizzards, firing stoves
to melt their ghosts.
                    Ours are no different,
except they melt us.

EARLY LESSONS

Lightning Bugs

It's possible to reach out in the night
and catch something flying so slow
it can be stopped in your small cupped hand
and on a hot night past bedtime, past rules
of winter, you can run
across the sprinkled grass
and your little fingers can close around wings
on the move, around light. Can trap it.
Can put it in a jar by your bed.
You drowse off under the click and hum
of the ceiling fan, the blink of small light.
It's all right to be small
in a white nightgown.

Peanut Brittle

Sweet voice you never forgot,
even at fifty, so high it's about to break
into something jagged and sharp,
hardened brown sugar:
honey, sweety, little lamb, now how's
your—is that your dollie? Isn't she pretty.
Aren't you pretty! Are you pretty?
You're so pretty.
You're so sweet.

Caution

It's best to huddle in the basement
during thunder. Lightning kills.
Spiders also are fatal. Cockroaches

will leave the room if you scream
loud enough. Loud enough, most dangers
will leave the room. Watch out
for men.

Soap Opera

The story that asks the question:
"Can a woman over thirty-five
find happiness?"
I was ten. At home again
with asthma and the radio.
Twenty-five years to go.

Books

From five I read
And read
And read
I'm not afraid
I am not dead

OVER MY HEAD

Over my head I hear a large black man;
between us is my ceiling and his floor.
It's been this way since I began

to come here, to try to understand
my life, my aging, my sad heart's core.
Over my head I hear a large black man

whose heavy footfalls shake my ceiling fan,
whose deep-throated voice shakes me even more.
It's been this way since I began

my fifties, looking for a place to plan
a life without desire or fear or guilt or
hearing over my head a large black man.

A Southern white woman, the best I can
do is hide what I no longer can ignore.
It's been this way since I began

to realize I'd like to touch his skin.
But I'll go in my room and close my door.
Over my head I hear a large black man.
It's been this way since I began.

Pictures with Cigarettes

Look closely:
Mother's pack of Luckies lies on the endtable,
See Dad's face against the baby's cheek?
The hand not lifting Tommy holds the smoke.
In this one, Grandpa's cigar smolders by the highchair
while Grandma holds her cigarette and wineglass
and a baby with one hand.

But this is not a tract; all these babies thrived,
survived their separate sorrows, bloomed
into periods of pure beauty, whole weeks
of unadulterated success, moments of total
attention from what seemed like all the world.
All still know results of love.

Of the smokers this is not a judgment,
only a report on mortal signs in pictures—
the scythe laid propped against the press,
the hourglass, sunset, drooping pheasant
replaced by cigarettes.
The pictured smokers are all gone,
not up in smoke, but somewhere we hope
they remember life as right in length
and without regrets.

RECORDED STORM

When the boy put his new tape recorder
on the window sill against the screen
it was a hot cloudy day.
Nothing was happening, yet. We
don't know what sound he was after—
birds maybe, wind, his parents on the porch.
(You remember when you had a camcorder
how you taped those hours of ordinary nothing?)

Now it's the only recording we have of
an attacking tornado—
(says the expert who doesn't report on the boy)
and it does sound, exactly as my father told me,
like a train.
Not its whistle; its wheels—
and you're on the trestle.

An on-off sound: chuff/off chuff/off
roar/off/roar.

Why trains sound like tornados or
tornados like trains must mean something
in our binary world.

That terrible yes-no warning, the SS
horn, most sinister of sirens,
careening to pick up the Franks;
your own loud heartbeat
drumming the pillow you've pressed
to muffle the angry house.

My mother and father heard it,
a sound they'd never heard before

but *like* a train.
They dropped to the floor.

They must have held each other then
—those two I never saw touch—
their hearts together in terror,
the pounding air bearing down.

They lost all but their lives
which continued long after,
love/hate swirling around them, off/on
the sound that announced them
wherever they went.
It was like that, *the tornado,*
he says of the freight train passing the hospice.
He looks at the window, not the machine
where her heart is depicted a blinking light.

My Daughter's Daughter
Takes to the Street

She's two, you turned your back, she's off—

as low to the ground as a pup and as slow, as quick
while you went inside for a sweater, came back
to the blank yard drained of its shapes by her absence.

You scan the street with desperate radar, run south
to scream her name across front yards—

Of two ways she could have gone you've chosen wrong.

In minutes other women leave their houses, one
takes the way you didn't guess she'd go. The woods,
the four-lane thoroughfare.

Of two ways she could have gone you've chosen wrong.

Bursting from the woods the neighbor sees
the baby lifted by a scruffy man into his pickup.

Of two ways this story could have gone . . .
it went right:
A good man saves the baby from the traffic,
a good woman carries her back home.

And now you're asking me to share your terror:
the ragged aftermath of nerve and breath.
You send your tremors to your mother
to take them in and shake when you hang up,
struck to the bone for what I know of choices:
that this relief's the least our bodies do.

ENTHUSIASM

Possessed by a god
says the word:
god is in.

Sure as a stroke
something spins in the brain,
fluttering the airy layers, taking over,
wreaking redness, wildness,
havoc in the actions.

Someone once made me ashamed of such mania.
It was after I'd had a baby.
Calm down, he said.

Rosy in the possible, I wonder
how the milkwhite understand anything.
They feint, they fend, they
palely duck the blow.

I was beside myself
Euripides wrote
through the voice
of the woman god-possessed.

She's not herself
is what I heard around here.
God—devoutly I wish now
to be pushed aside.

Come on, come in,
knock me out.

UNBALANCED

Winter, 1995

Accurate languages
fragged into that side and this
atomized over the damaged maps

this little globe grows
more and more home
until Chechnya and Zagreb
shadow the optimistic grass
of Gettysburg

and here
unheard-of murders
become what one could do

until one night walking
on the swinging bridge thinner than feet
your outstretched upturned palms
depending
as always on even rain
you're surprised by one hand dry.

You would plunge but for poetry
or whatever the better word
for when language composes
the drifting chips of the world's
composure, fills the empty
outstretched hand with flakes
that counterweigh the one with rain.

THE STATESMAN

You're going to die before I am.
But even that statement is
under suspicion;
those crab cells in your stomach
can't move as fast as the car
sweeping the curve on Three Chopt Road
that will hit me head on and leave
me splattered and random
on no road of my own.

Do I envy your exit?
You have moved like a statesman
into your long negotiation with death.
I can picture you a man in a Saville Row coat,
an expensive conservative hat. Dignified,
tall, you stride into the chosen place—
Potsdam, Yalta, the end of a pier
on the Rappahannock—and it's clear
you hold all the cards.

So much of courage is posture.
The straight spine, the lifted chin, you
have never failed to project. Yet
as one more month crumbles into another,
I practice your pain as you dress for the day—
and wonder if ever
you've sneaked in your nightgown
down to the curve on Three Chopt Road.

The statesman is discreet; the treaty
you wrought is held in trust
in your secret heart. But your documents—
oh, your papers are art—
and you've left these unsealed, for us.

ENGAGEMENT DAY

for Matt and Betsy

October sun fullbeam out of the golden Blue Ridge
up over Afton flooding the Shenandoah Valley,
sharpening the edges of red barns on blue sky.
What a day of sons and daughters!
The perfect baby set plump and plumb in the middle
of the sunlit meadow. Simple as infant and field,
all imperfect adults easy in and out of sweaters,
all the old ravelments knitted into autumn,
gentled into beige and russet and gold
like the old Alleghenies giving up thick
drooping green, staving off the iced grays, for this
warm wedge of color and mild air, this bright quilt
under the blue sky's sun. And my son
shining at the tall young woman looking over at Jump
Mountain, telling us the story of the Indian pair
who jumped for love and there we are,
families, family, the baby
in the middle of the hilltop meadow
graced in sunlight and this rare jump of love.

LEAVING THE BUTTERFLY BUSH

You have to have seen one to know at first
the eight-foot bush isn't full of windwaved flames
or shards of thin stained glass
firing the sunlight to orange and gold.

The monarchs are migrating,
gathering in the Blue Ridge to feast and fill
on aster and goldenrod and especially buddleia,
the fragrant violet butterfly bush.
They'll fatten in late summer sun, then fly
three thousand miles to Mexico.

Now among the heavy August greens,
this hillside's dotted with their fluttering
and here and there an early dying leaf,
a thin yellow walnut leaf,
briefly becomes a butterfly.

I want to take a picture of my lively buddleia
for I must go down the mountain now
and when I return the monarchs will have flown,
the purple spikes sucked dry and browned.

But I have no camera—and what if I did?—
it is the movement that amazes.
And no video could do it, missing the scent,
the silence, the feel of the Long Mountain air
on my skin—as if I'm being softly fanned
by a thousand pairs of wings without a sound.

I can't preserve this moment
any more than Moses could—
just watch a bush ignited,
and try to write it down.